Scarf Patterns for Beginners

A Guide Book to Cozy Warmth through Knitting

Harvey G Carlos

THIS BOOK BELONGS TO
The Library of

....

....

Did you like my book? I pondered it severely before releasing this book. Although the response has been overwhelming, it is always pleasing to see, read or hear a new comment. Thank you for reading this and I would love to hear your honest opinion about it. Furthermore, many people are searching for a unique book, and your feedback will help me gather the right books for my reading audience.

Thanks!

Table of Contents

SUMMARY

HOW TO: CAST ON, KNIT, PURL, AND BIND OFF: In this tutorial, we will guide you through the step-by-step process of casting on, knitting, purling, and binding off. These fundamental techniques are essential for any beginner knitter and will serve as the foundation for more complex knitting projects.

First, let's start with casting on. Casting on is the process of creating the first row of stitches on your knitting needle. There are various methods of casting on, but the most common one is the long-tail cast on. To begin, make a slipknot by creating a loop with the yarn and pulling the tail through. Slide this loop onto your knitting needle, leaving a long tail of yarn hanging down. Hold the needle with the slipknot in your right hand and the tail in your left hand. With your right hand, insert the needle into the loop from left to right, then wrap the yarn around the needle counterclockwise. Pull the loop through the slipknot, creating a new stitch on your needle. Repeat this process until you have the desired number of stitches.

Once you have cast on your stitches, you are ready to start knitting. Knitting involves creating new stitches by pulling loops of yarn through existing stitches. Hold the needle with the stitches in your left hand and the empty needle in your right hand. Insert the right needle into the first stitch on the left needle, going from left to right. Wrap the yarn counterclockwise around the right needle, then use the right needle to pull the loop of yarn through the stitch, slipping the stitch off the left needle. You have now created a new stitch on your right needle. Repeat this process for each stitch until all the stitches have been transferred to the right needle.

Next, let's move on to purling. Purling is the opposite of knitting and creates a different texture on your fabric. Hold the needle with the stitches in your left hand and the empty needle in your right hand. Insert the right needle into the first stitch on the left needle, this time going from right to left. Wrap the yarn counterclockwise around the right needle, then use the right needle to pull the loop of yarn through the stitch, slipping the stitch off the left needle. You have now purled a stitch. Repeat this process for each stitch until all the stitches have been transferred to the right needle.

The Joy and Utility of Hand-Knit Scarves in Knitting: Hand-knit scarves are not only a joy to create but also serve as a highly practical and versatile accessory in the world of knitting. The process of knitting a scarf by hand allows for a unique and personal touch, making each piece a one-of-a-kind creation. From selecting the perfect yarn to mastering various knitting techniques, the journey of creating a hand-knit scarf is a fulfilling and rewarding experience.

One of the greatest joys of hand-knitting a scarf is the ability to choose from a wide range of yarns. Knitters have the freedom to select yarns of different colors, textures, and fibers, allowing for endless possibilities in creating a scarf that perfectly matches their personal style and preferences. Whether it's a soft and cozy merino wool for a winter scarf or a lightweight cotton blend for a summer accessory, the choice of yarn can greatly enhance the overall look and feel of the finished scarf.

Furthermore, the process of knitting a scarf by hand provides an opportunity to explore and master various knitting techniques. From basic stitches like knit and purl to more intricate patterns such as cables and lace, the possibilities for creativity are endless. Each stitch and pattern adds a unique texture and visual interest to the scarf, making it a true work of art. Knitters can experiment with different stitch combinations and patterns, creating a scarf that is not only beautiful but also showcases their knitting skills.

Hand-knit scarves also offer a level of customization that is hard to find in store-bought accessories. Knitters can adjust the length and width of the scarf to their liking, ensuring a perfect fit. Additionally, they can add personalized details such as fringe, tassels, or even embroidery, making the scarf truly unique and reflective of their individual style. This level of customization allows for a sense of pride and ownership over the finished product, making it a cherished item that can be passed down through generations.

In addition to being a joy to create, hand-knit scarves are also highly practical and versatile. They provide warmth and protection during colder months, making them an essential accessory for braving the winter chill. The thickness and weight of the yarn can be adjusted to suit different climates, ensuring that the scarf is comfortable to wear in any weather. Moreover, hand-knit scarves can be styled in a variety of ways, from draping it loosely around the neck to wrapping it snugly for added warmth. This versatility allows for endless possibilities in creating different looks and outfits.

How to Navigate and Use This Guidebook in Knitting: Welcome to the guidebook on knitting! This comprehensive guide is designed to help you navigate through the world of knitting and provide you with all the necessary information and techniques to become a skilled knitter.

To make the most out of this guidebook, it is important to understand how it is structured and how to effectively use it. The guidebook is divided into several sections, each focusing on different aspects of knitting. Let's take a closer look at each section and how you can navigate through them.

1. Introduction: This section provides a brief overview of knitting, its history, and its various applications. It is a great starting point for beginners who are new to knitting and want to gain a basic understanding of the craft.

2. Tools and Materials: In this section, you will learn about the essential tools and materials needed for knitting. From knitting needles and yarns to stitch markers and tapestry needles, this section will guide you through the different options available and help you choose the right tools for your projects.

3. Basic Techniques: Here, you will find step-by-step instructions on the fundamental knitting techniques. From casting on and knitting stitches to purling, increasing, and decreasing, this section covers all the basics you need to know to get started with knitting.

4. Advanced Techniques: Once you have mastered the basic techniques, this section will introduce you to more advanced knitting techniques. From cable knitting and lace knitting to colorwork and intarsia, you will learn how to create intricate patterns and textures in your knitting projects.

5. Patterns and Projects: This section is dedicated to providing you with a variety of knitting patterns and projects to practice your skills. From simple scarves and hats to more complex sweaters and blankets, you will find a range of projects suitable for different skill levels.

6. Troubleshooting: Knitting can sometimes be challenging, especially for beginners. This section addresses common knitting problems and provides solutions to help you overcome any difficulties you may encounter along the way.

To effectively use this guidebook, it is recommended to start from the beginning and work your way through each section in order. However, feel free to jump to specific sections that interest you or address your current needs. The guidebook is designed to be flexible and cater to knitters of all levels.

Throughout the guidebook, you will find clear and concise instructions, accompanied by illustrations and diagrams to help you visualize each step. Take your time to read and understand each technique before moving on to the next.

Getting Acquainted with Knitting Tools and Materials in Knitting: When it comes to knitting, it is essential to familiarize yourself with the various tools and materials that are commonly used in this craft. Understanding the purpose and function of each item will not only make your knitting experience more enjoyable but also help you achieve better results in your projects.

One of the most basic tools you will need is knitting needles. These come in different sizes and materials, such as metal, wood, or plastic. The size of the needles determines the gauge or tension of your knitting, with smaller needles producing tighter stitches and larger needles creating looser stitches. It is important to choose the right size needles for your project, as this will affect the overall size and drape of your knitted item.

Another essential tool is a crochet hook. While primarily used for crochet, a crochet hook can also come in handy in knitting. It can be used to fix mistakes, pick up dropped stitches, or create decorative elements like picot edges. Having a crochet hook in your knitting toolkit will save you time and frustration when dealing with any unexpected issues that may arise during your project.

Yarn is, of course, the main material used in knitting. Yarn comes in a wide variety of fibers, weights, and colors, each with its own unique characteristics. The fiber content of the yarn will determine its softness, warmth, and durability. Common yarn fibers include wool, cotton, acrylic, and blends of these materials. The weight of the yarn refers to its thickness, with thinner yarns being classified as lace or fingering weight, and thicker yarns falling into categories like worsted or bulky weight. Choosing the right yarn for your project is crucial, as it will affect the overall look and feel of your finished piece.

In addition to knitting needles and yarn, there are several other tools that can enhance your knitting experience. Stitch markers are small rings or clips that can be placed on your knitting needles to mark specific stitches or sections of your pattern. These markers help you keep track of your progress and ensure that you are following the pattern correctly. Tapestry needles are used for weaving in loose ends and sewing pieces of your knitted project together. They have a large eye and a blunt tip, making them easy to thread and maneuver through your stitches.

Measuring tools, such as a tape measure or ruler, are essential for checking your gauge and ensuring that your knitted item will fit properly. Blocking tools, such as blocking mats and pins, are used to shape and set your finished knitted

Mastering Basic Knitting Stitches and Techniques in Knitting: Mastering Basic Knitting Stitches and Techniques in Knitting is a comprehensive guide that aims to equip beginners with the necessary skills and knowledge to become proficient in the art of knitting. This guide covers a wide range of topics, including the fundamental stitches and techniques that form the foundation of knitting.

The guide begins by introducing the reader to the basic tools and materials needed for knitting. It provides a detailed explanation of each tool, such as knitting needles, yarn, and stitch markers, and offers tips on how to choose the right materials for different projects. This section also includes information on how to properly hold the knitting needles and tension the yarn, ensuring that beginners start off on the right foot.

Once the reader is familiar with the tools and materials, the guide delves into the various knitting stitches. It starts with the most basic stitch, the knit stitch, and provides step-by-step instructions on how to execute it correctly. The guide then progresses to more advanced stitches, such as the purl stitch, the stockinette stitch, and the garter stitch. Each stitch is explained in detail, with accompanying diagrams and photos to aid understanding.

In addition to the basic stitches, the guide also covers a variety of knitting techniques. It explores techniques such as casting on, binding off, increasing, and decreasing, which are essential for shaping and creating different patterns in knitting. The guide provides clear instructions and illustrations for each technique, ensuring that beginners can easily follow along and practice.

To further enhance the learning experience, the guide includes a collection of beginner-friendly knitting patterns. These patterns are designed to help beginners practice their newly acquired skills and create beautiful projects.

From scarves and hats to blankets and sweaters, the patterns cover a wide range of items that are both practical and stylish.

Throughout the guide, there are also helpful tips and tricks provided by experienced knitters. These tips offer valuable insights and advice on common mistakes to avoid, troubleshooting techniques, and ways to improve knitting speed and efficiency. The guide also addresses common challenges that beginners may face, such as dropped stitches and uneven tension, and offers solutions to overcome these obstacles.

By the end of Mastering Basic Knitting Stitches and Techniques in Knitting, beginners will have gained a solid foundation in knitting. They will have mastered the essential stitches and techniques, and will be able to confidently tackle more complex knitting projects. Whether they aspire to create intricate lace patterns or cozy winter accessories, this guide will serve as a valuable resource for anyone looking to embark on their

The Ways Reading and Understanding Knitting Patterns: Reading and understanding knitting patterns can be a challenging task for beginners, but with practice and patience, it becomes easier over time. Knitting patterns are essentially a set of instructions that guide you through the process of creating a specific knitted item, such as a sweater, hat, or scarf. They provide you with the necessary information regarding the type of yarn to use, the size of the needles, and the specific stitches and techniques required to complete the project.

One of the first things to consider when reading a knitting pattern is the skill level required. Patterns are often categorized as beginner, intermediate, or advanced, indicating the level of difficulty involved. It is important to choose a pattern that matches your skill level to ensure a successful outcome. Beginners should start with simple patterns that use basic stitches and techniques, while more experienced knitters can challenge themselves with complex patterns that incorporate advanced stitches and techniques.

Next, it is crucial to carefully read through the entire pattern before starting the project. This allows you to familiarize yourself with the overall structure and understand the different sections and abbreviations used. Knitting patterns often include a list of materials needed, gauge information, and specific instructions for each section of the project. Taking the time to thoroughly understand the pattern will help prevent mistakes and confusion later on.

Understanding the abbreviations and symbols used in knitting patterns is another key aspect of reading and interpreting them correctly. Knitting patterns often use shorthand abbreviations to represent different stitches and techniques. For example, k stands for knit stitch, p stands for purl stitch, and yo stands for yarn over. It is essential to refer to the pattern's key or glossary to familiarize yourself with these abbreviations and symbols. This will enable you to follow the instructions accurately and achieve the desired outcome.

Additionally, paying attention to the gauge information provided in the pattern is crucial for achieving the correct size and fit of the finished item. Gauge refers to the number of stitches and rows per inch in a knitted fabric. It is important to match the gauge specified in the pattern by using the recommended yarn and needle size. Failing to achieve the correct gauge can result in a finished item that is either too small or too large. To ensure accuracy, it is recommended to create a gauge swatch before starting the project. This involves knitting a small sample using the recommended yarn and needle size and measuring the number of stitches and rows per inch. Adjustments can then be made by changing the needle size until the

Organizing Your Knitting Space and Supplies: Organizing your knitting space and supplies is essential for a smooth and enjoyable knitting experience. A well-organized space not only helps you find your materials easily but also allows you to work efficiently and stay focused on your projects. Whether you have a dedicated knitting room or a small corner in your living room, here are some tips to help you create an organized and functional knitting space.

Firstly, assess your current knitting space and take note of any areas that need improvement. Look for cluttered surfaces, tangled yarns, and disorganized storage. Once you have identified the problem areas, you can start planning how to optimize your space.

One of the first steps in organizing your knitting space is to declutter. Sort through your knitting supplies and get rid of any items that you no longer use or need. This includes old or unfinished projects, duplicate needles, and yarns that you don't love anymore. By decluttering, you will create more space and make it easier to find the materials you actually use.

Next, consider investing in storage solutions that suit your needs. There are various options available, such as baskets, bins, shelves, and drawers. Choose storage containers that are sturdy, easily accessible, and can accommodate your knitting supplies. For example, clear plastic bins are great for storing yarns as they allow you to see the colors and textures at a glance. Utilize vertical space by installing shelves or hanging organizers to maximize storage capacity.

To keep your yarns tangle-free and easily accessible, consider using yarn organizers or a yarn swift. These tools help to keep your yarns neatly wound and prevent them from getting tangled or damaged. Additionally, using clear plastic bags or ziplock bags to store individual projects can help keep everything organized and prevent any mix-ups.

Another important aspect of organizing your knitting space is creating a designated workspace. This can be a table, desk, or even a comfortable chair with a side table. Make sure your workspace is well-lit and has enough room for your knitting projects. Keep essential tools, such as scissors, stitch markers, and tapestry needles, within reach to avoid constant interruptions while knitting.

Labeling is also a helpful technique to keep your knitting supplies organized. Use labels or tags to identify different types of yarn, needle sizes, and project bags. This will save you time and frustration when searching for specific items.

Tips for Choosing the Right Yarns and Needles in Knitting: When it comes to knitting, choosing the right yarns and needles is crucial for achieving the desired results in your projects. With so many options available in the market, it can be overwhelming to make the right choice. However, by considering a few key factors, you can ensure that you select the perfect yarn and needles for your knitting endeavors.

Firstly, it is important to understand the different types of yarns available. Yarns come in various fibers, such as wool, cotton, acrylic, and blends of these materials. Each fiber has its own unique characteristics, which can greatly impact the final outcome of your knitting project. For example, wool yarns are known for their warmth and elasticity, making them ideal for winter garments and accessories. On the other hand, cotton yarns are lightweight and breathable, making them suitable for summer wear. Acrylic yarns, on the other hand, are often chosen for their affordability and easy care. By considering the purpose of your project and the qualities you desire in your finished piece, you can narrow down your options and choose the most suitable yarn.

In addition to fiber, the weight or thickness of the yarn is another important consideration. Yarns are categorized into different weights, ranging from lace weight to super bulky. The weight of the yarn will determine the size of the stitches and the overall drape of your project. For intricate lacework or delicate garments, a lace or fingering weight yarn would be appropriate. For cozy blankets or chunky sweaters, a bulky or super bulky weight yarn would be more suitable. It is important to match the weight of the yarn to the pattern you are using, as using a different weight can alter the size and proportions of your project.

Once you have chosen the yarn, selecting the right needles is equally important. Needles come in various materials, such as metal, wood, and plastic. Each material has its own advantages and disadvantages. Metal needles are known for their smoothness and durability, making them ideal for fast knitters or those working with slippery yarns. Wood needles, on the other hand, have a natural warmth and grip, making them comfortable to hold and suitable for those with hand or joint issues. Plastic needles are often the most affordable option and are lightweight, making them suitable for beginners or those on a budget. It is important to consider your personal preferences and knitting style when choosing the material of your needles.

Combining Different Stitches and Techniques in Knitting: Combining different stitches and techniques in knitting allows for endless possibilities and creativity in your projects. By incorporating various stitches, you can create unique textures, patterns, and designs that will make your knitted items stand out.

One way to combine different stitches is by using a stitch pattern. A stitch pattern is a sequence of stitches that are repeated throughout a row or round. This can be as simple as alternating between knit and purl stitches, or as complex as incorporating lace or cable stitches. By following a stitch pattern, you can create intricate designs that add visual interest to your knitting.

Another technique for combining stitches is colorwork. Colorwork involves using multiple colors of yarn to create patterns or images in your knitting. This can be done through techniques such as stranded knitting, intarsia, or slip stitch colorwork. By combining different colors and stitches, you can create stunning and vibrant designs that will make your knitted items truly unique.

In addition to stitch patterns and colorwork, you can also combine different techniques in your knitting. For example, you can incorporate lace knitting into a cable pattern, or add a textured stitch to a stockinette stitch background. By combining different techniques, you can create multidimensional and visually appealing knitted items.

When combining different stitches and techniques, it is important to consider the overall design and purpose of your project. Think about how the different stitches and techniques will work together to achieve the desired effect. Experiment with swatches and samples to see how the stitches and techniques interact with each other before committing to a larger project.

Furthermore, it is essential to have a good understanding of the stitches and techniques you are using. Take the time to learn and practice each stitch and technique individually before attempting to combine them. This will ensure that you have a solid foundation and will help you avoid any mistakes or frustrations along the way.

Lastly, don't be afraid to get creative and think outside the box when combining different stitches and techniques. Knitting is a versatile craft that allows for endless possibilities. Explore different stitch patterns, experiment with color combinations, and try out new techniques to create truly unique and personalized knitted items.

In conclusion, combining different stitches and techniques in knitting opens up a world of possibilities for creativity and design. By incorporating stitch patterns, colorwork, and various techniques, you can create visually stunning and unique knitted items. Take the time to learn and practice each stitch and technique, and don't be afraid to experiment and think outside the box. With patience and

Exploring Different Scarf Lengths and Widths in Knitting: When it comes to knitting scarves, there are endless possibilities in terms of length and width. The choice of scarf length and width can greatly impact the overall look and functionality of the finished piece. Whether you prefer a short and wide scarf or a long and narrow one, experimenting with different dimensions can lead to unique and personalized creations.

One of the first considerations when deciding on scarf length is the intended purpose of the accessory. A shorter scarf, typically around 50-60 inches in length, is perfect for adding a touch of style to an outfit without overwhelming the wearer. This length is ideal for draping around the neck once or twice, creating a cozy and fashionable look. It is also a great option for those who prefer a more minimalistic approach to scarf wearing.

On the other hand, a longer scarf, ranging from 70-80 inches or even longer, offers more versatility in terms of styling. This length allows for various wrapping techniques, such as the classic loop around the neck or the trendy infinity style. A longer scarf can also be worn as a shawl or even used as a blanket in chilly environments. The extra length provides warmth and comfort, making it a popular choice for those living in colder climates.

When it comes to scarf width, there are also several factors to consider. A wider scarf, typically around 8-10 inches, offers more coverage and can be wrapped around the neck multiple times for added warmth. This width is perfect for chunky yarns or intricate stitch patterns that showcase the texture of the scarf. It also allows for more creativity in terms of draping and styling, as the extra fabric can be manipulated in various ways.

On the other hand, a narrower scarf, around 4-6 inches in width, offers a more streamlined and elegant look. This width is ideal for lightweight yarns or delicate stitch patterns that create a more delicate and airy scarf. A narrower scarf can be worn as a simple accessory, adding a touch of color or pattern to an outfit without overwhelming the wearer. It is also a great option for those who prefer a more minimalist or understated style.

In addition to length and width, the choice of yarn and stitch pattern can also greatly impact the overall look and feel of the scarf. Thicker yarns and more intricate stitch patterns tend to create a bulkier and warmer scarf, while thinner yarns and simpler stitch patterns result in a lighter and more delicate accessory.

Ultimately, the choice of scarf length and width in knitting is

Adjusting Patterns to Suit Your Preferences in Knitting: When it comes to knitting, one of the most exciting aspects is the ability to adjust patterns to suit your own preferences. Whether you're a beginner or an experienced knitter, being able to customize a pattern can truly elevate your knitting experience and allow you to create unique and personalized pieces.

One of the first steps in adjusting a knitting pattern is understanding the different elements that make up the design. This includes the stitch pattern, the gauge, and the sizing. By familiarizing yourself with these components, you can begin to make modifications that will suit your preferences.

The stitch pattern refers to the specific combination of stitches used in a pattern. This can range from simple knit and purl stitches to more intricate lace or cable patterns. If you find a pattern that you love but aren't a fan of the stitch pattern, don't be afraid to switch it up. You can easily substitute a different stitch pattern that you prefer, as long as you maintain the same number of stitches and rows.

Gauge is another important factor to consider when adjusting a knitting pattern. Gauge refers to the number of stitches and rows per inch that you achieve with a specific yarn and needle size. It is crucial to match the gauge specified in the pattern in order to ensure that your finished piece will have the correct measurements. However, if you prefer a looser or tighter fabric, you can adjust your needle size accordingly. Just be sure to knit a gauge swatch before starting your project to ensure that your adjustments will result in the desired measurements.

Sizing is yet another aspect that can be adjusted to suit your preferences. Most knitting patterns provide instructions for multiple sizes, allowing you to choose the one that best fits your measurements. However, if you fall in between sizes or prefer a different fit, you can easily make modifications. This can involve adding or subtracting stitches or rows, or even adjusting the shaping of the garment. Just be sure to keep track of your modifications and make any necessary adjustments throughout the pattern.

In addition to these technical adjustments, you can also personalize a knitting pattern through the choice of yarn and color. Yarn selection can greatly impact the drape, texture, and overall look of your finished piece. Experimenting with different yarns can help you achieve the desired effect and make the pattern truly your own. Similarly, choosing different colors or color combinations can add a unique touch to your knitting project.

Mending and Caring for Your Hand-Knits in Knitting: Mending and caring for your hand-knits is an essential part of maintaining their longevity and ensuring that they continue to look their best. Hand-knitted items, whether they are sweaters, scarves, or hats, require special attention and care to keep them in top condition.

One of the most common issues that hand-knitted items face is the occurrence of small holes or snags. These can happen due to regular wear and tear or accidental mishaps. The good news is that these issues can be easily fixed with a few simple techniques. The first step is to identify the hole or snag and assess its size and severity. For smaller holes, you can use a technique called duplicate stitching, where you essentially recreate the missing stitches using a darning needle and matching yarn. This method is great for repairing small holes without compromising the overall look of the garment.

For larger holes or more extensive damage, you may need to consider a technique called patching. This involves using a piece of matching yarn or fabric to cover the damaged area and secure it in place with careful stitching. Patching can be a bit more time-consuming, but it is a great way to salvage a beloved hand-knit item that may otherwise be deemed unwearable.

In addition to mending, proper care is crucial for maintaining the quality and appearance of your hand-knits. One of the most important steps is to follow the washing instructions provided by the yarn manufacturer. Hand-knitted items are often made from delicate fibers that require gentle handling. Avoid using harsh detergents or washing machines, as they can cause damage or shrinkage. Instead, opt for hand-washing in lukewarm water with a mild detergent specifically designed for delicate fabrics.

After washing, it is important to reshape your hand-knitted items to their original dimensions. Gently squeeze out excess water and lay the item flat on a clean towel. Use your hands to carefully stretch and shape the garment back to its intended size. Avoid wringing or twisting the fabric, as this can cause it to lose its shape.

Drying your hand-knits is another crucial step in their care routine. Lay them flat on a clean, dry towel or a mesh drying rack, making sure to reshape them as necessary. Avoid hanging them up to dry, as this can cause stretching or distortion. Allow them to air dry naturally, away from direct sunlight or heat sources.

Lastly, proper storage is essential for preserving the quality of your hand-k

CHAPTER 1: HOW TO: CAST ON, KNIT, PURL, AND BIND OFF

Every knitting project imaginable, from complexly cabled socks to lacy stoles, to chunky scarves, are built on four basic processes: casting on (putting new stitches on the needle), knitting, purling, and binding off (securing the stitches at the end of the work). Realistically, knitting and purling are two ways of creating the same stitch – the difference lies in which way the 'bump' of the old stitch pushed. Although there are an almost infinite number of ways to perform these four basic processes, some better suited for making scarves than others, any aspiring knitters who learn to perform these four actions (even in their most basic forms) can produce as many scarves as they desire.

New knitters might wonder if knit and purl are basically the same stitch and what is the difference between the two? When a new stitch is created, the stitch from the previous row must go somewhere; it is pushed to either one side of the fabric or the other. This bump can be placed at the back of the fabric (the side facing away from the knitter's body) or it can be placed at the front of the fabric (the side facing the knitter's body). When knitters do the first, moving the bump to the back, they are knitting; when knitters do the second, moving the bump to the front, they are purling.

Patterns direct knitters to knit or purl in order to make designs or types of fabric. Depending on how the bumps are artfully placed and arranged to the front and back sides, an endless array of designs can be created. Stockinette stitch, for example, is one of the most common fabrics created by knitters. Every purl bump is pushed to one side of the fabric, which creates the characteristic smooth and bumpy sides of the fabric. To create this fabric, all a knitter must do is alternate between knit and purl rows – simple, yet useful.

Of course, before any stitches can be knit or purled, new stitches need to be placed on the needle. This is the cast on. Many types of cast ons are available to knitters, some plain, some fancy, some elastic, some tight. One all-purpose cast on is the long-tail cast on. Although there are simpler cast ons, the long-tail has few drawbacks and can be memorized with a little practice.

The Long-Tail Cast On

The long-tail cast on is so named because a long 'tail' of yarn is used to create the stitches. This means that before beginning to work the cast on, the knitter must pull enough yarn free to create the number of stitches desired. For a small amount of stitches, perhaps under 30, a 12- to 18-inch tail is most likely sufficient. There is no exact formula for estimating the amount of yarn tail needed, but knitters who have more than sufficient yarn for the project might make the tail extra long to avoid having to start over.

First, the knitter readies for the cast on by pulling yarn free for the long tail. Then, the knitter places the yarn over the thumb and index finger of the left hand; the tail should lie over the thumb and the working yarn over the index finger. The two strands of yarn are gripped with the rest of the fingers:

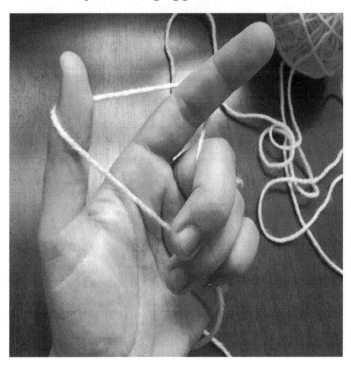

Next, the knitter inserts the needle under the yarn and pulls it slightly toward the body:

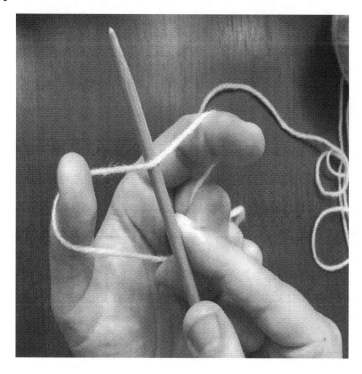

The needle goes under the yarn on the thumb, pulling it up:

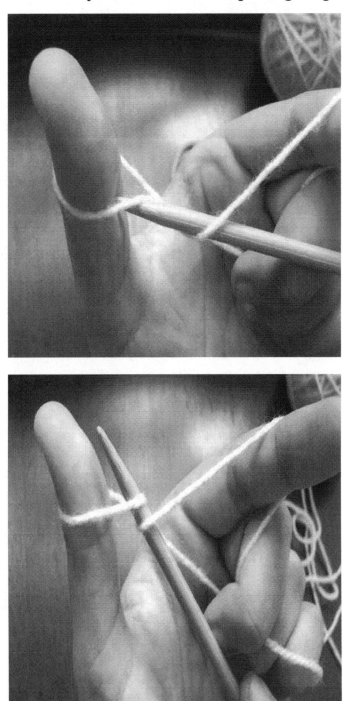

Then the needle goes over the yarn on the index finger, pulling it up and through the space that was created:

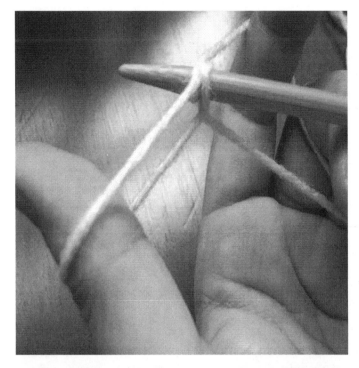

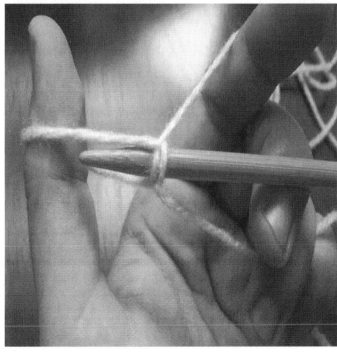

Now the knitter cinches the two stitches around the needle, but not too tightly:

After the first two stitches are created, the knitter is ready to begin again by placing the tail over the thumb, the working yarn over the index finger, and completing the same motions. Note that after the initial two stitches are made, only one stitch will be made with each motion:

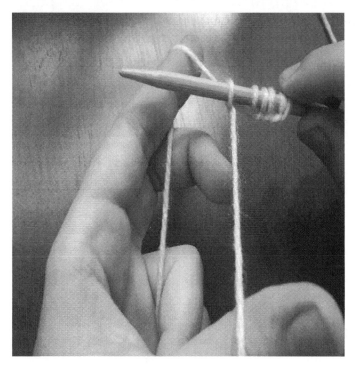

Once the desired number of stitches has been reached, the knitter has one complete cast on row. This row counts as one knit row of stitches.

The Knit Stitch

The knit stitch pushes the bumps to the back of the fabric. Knitters who are first starting to work the knit stitch should remember to aim for an even tension – after each stitch, the yarn is gently tugged to draw up any slack in the stitch, but not pulled so tightly that the stitch 'strangles' the needle.

First, the knitter holds the needle with the cast on stitches in the left hand and the empty needle in the right hand. The working yarn should be at the stitch at the tip of the needle:

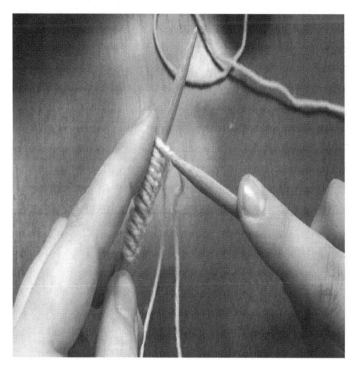

Next, the knitter inserts the tip of the empty needle into the first stitch on the left needle. The needle should enter the stitch from the bottom, i.e., the side closest to the rest of the stitches:

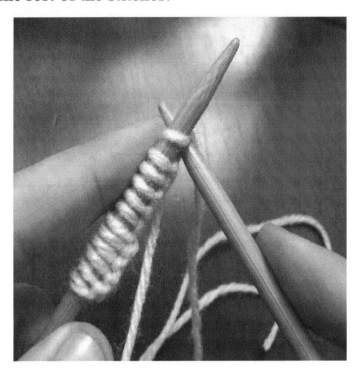

Now the knitter wraps the yarn around the right needle with the right hand *counterclockwise*:

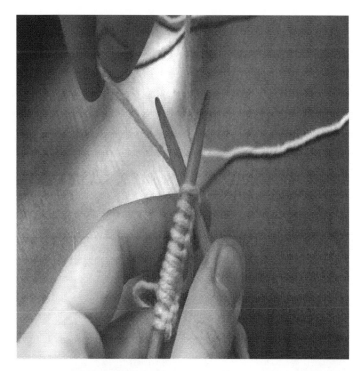

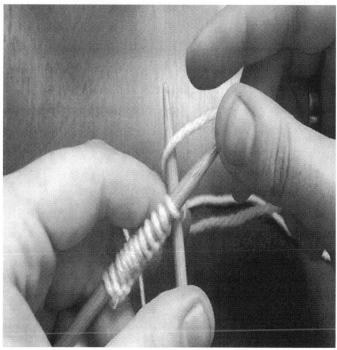

Then, the knitter pulls the right needle through the old stitch, catching the new one:

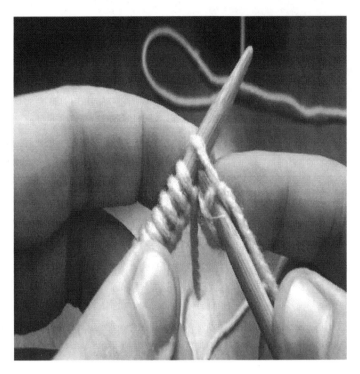

The old stitch is gently pulled off the left needle. These actions are repeated for each stitch across the needle:

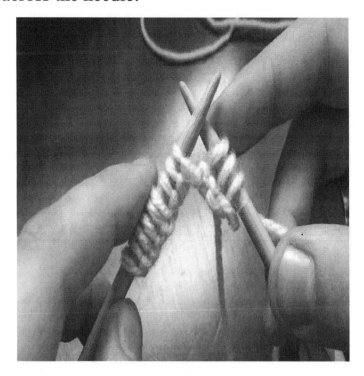

Once the last stitch is finished, the needles change hands, and the next row can be started. As knitters are starting out, they should be careful not to knit with the yarn tail, always picking up the working yarn (the yarn coming off the ball) instead.

One note about holding the working yarn: There is no right or wrong way. Many beginning knitters, however, pick up and drop the yarn as they need it. Although this isn't wrong per se, holding the yarn with the fingers of the right hand makes the process faster. One common way of holding the yarn is to loop it over the index finger:

Ultimately, though, the way that feels most comfortable is perfectly fine. The same goes for holding the working yarn while purling.

The Purl Stitch

New knitters often have a fear of working the purl stitch, hearing from experienced knitters that it is more 'difficult' or 'awkward.' This simply doesn't have to be true; remember, they're fundamentally the same stitch, even if worked differently, and with a little practice, the purl stitch will feel just as natural as the knit stitch.

First, the knitter holds the yarn and needles in the same manner as for a knit stitch – needle with stitches in the left hand, empty needle in the right hand. Next, the knitter inserts the right needle into the first stitch on the left needle. This time the right needle enters from top to bottom, i.e., from the side nearest the tip. The working yarn should be toward the front:

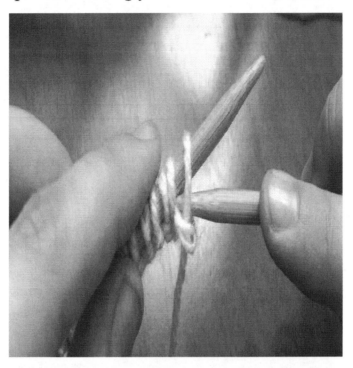

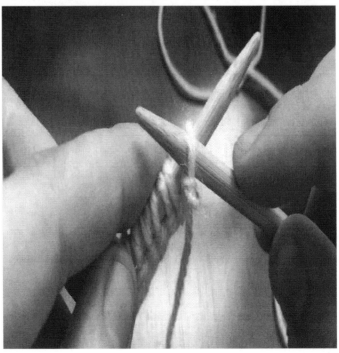

Now the knitter wraps the yarn around the needle *counterclockwise*:

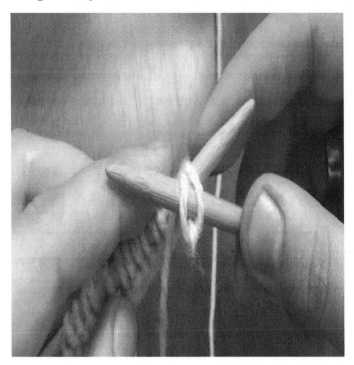

Then, the knitter draws the new stitch through the old one:

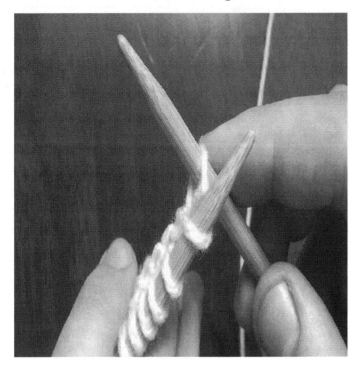

The knitter pulls the old stitch off the left needle; one purl stitch is finished and the knitter continues across the row:

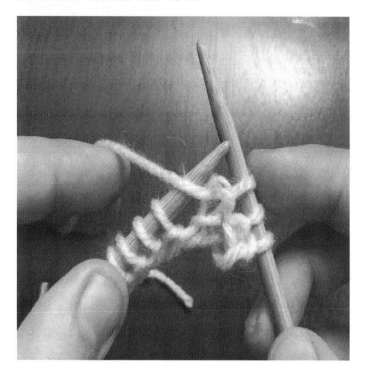

When the end of the row is reached, the needles change hands and a new row is begun.

At the beginning of each purl row, knitters should be careful not to fall into one common 'trap' of purling: working the new purl stitch into the stitch of the previous row, not the one being worked.

Here's how the stitch should look at the beginning of the purl row:

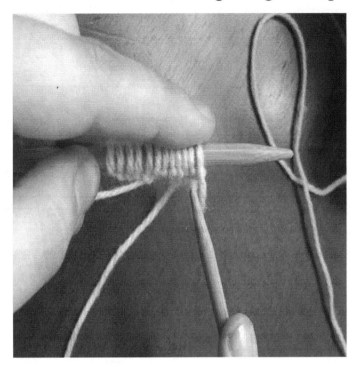

Here's how it will look if the yarn is pulled to the back, bringing up the stitch from the row below:

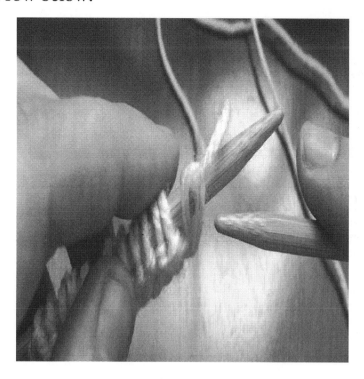

If the two bars of the stitch from the row below are worked (instead of the one bar of the current row's stitch), the knitter will increase one stitch on the row. Each time a purl row is begun, new knitters should check to ensure that they're working the correct stitch.

The Bind Off

Luckily, the bind off is the easiest of the four basic processes – new knitters can take a deep breath knowing that the last step isn't the most difficult! This is the all-purpose, basic bind off, the one knitters use when a pattern doesn't specify a different type of bind off.

First, the knitter knits the first two stitches in the row:

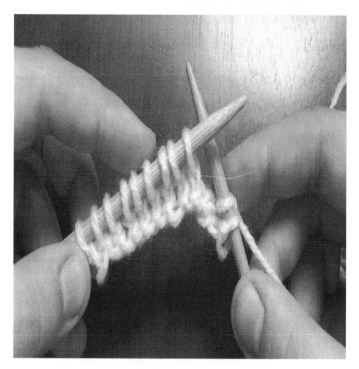

Then, the knitter inserts the tip of the left needle into the stitch on the right needle that is further from the tip:

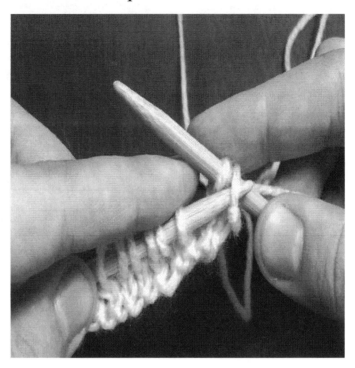

Now the knitter gently pulls this stich over the stitch closer to the tip, then off the needle:

Ready to begin again, the knitter knits a new stitch, and the process is repeated to the end of the row:

When only the last stitch remains on the right needle, the knitter can cut the yarn and draw it through the stitch to secure it.

At any one time, there should only be a maximum of two stitches on the right needle. As the knitter works the bind off, the stitches can be snugged, but not too tightly. The bind off has a tendency to be tighter than the cast on, so if the bind off row is worked with a very rigid tension, the two ends of the work will not match.

Note, that the bind off can be worked in purl or knit. To work the bind off in purl, the stitches are purled across the row. When a pattern directs the knitter to 'bind off in pattern,' the stitches should be knit or purled for the bind off according to the way they've been worked in the pattern (so, for example, a pattern alternating between knit and purl stitches would be bound off in the same manner).

CHAPTER 2: BEYOND THE BASICS

Once knitters feel comfortable working the knit and purl stitches, they are ready to try new techniques, all of which are variations of knit and purl. The following is by no means an exhaustive list of every stitch variation and technique available to knitters; these are, instead, the 'next step' basics, the techniques beginners should learn once they've conquered the four main processes. The scarf patterns found at the end of this book make use of these techniques, so once a knitter has learned to work them, he or she has the skills necessary to begin creating knitted scarves.

Knit Through the Back Loop

Knitting through the back loop of a stitch creates a twisted stitch, one that is tighter and often used because of its visual interest. This stitch is generally abbreviated 'ktbl' in patterns.

First, the knitter prepares to work a stitch as normal. Then, instead of sliding the needle though the front leg of the stitch, the knitter slides the needle through the back leg:

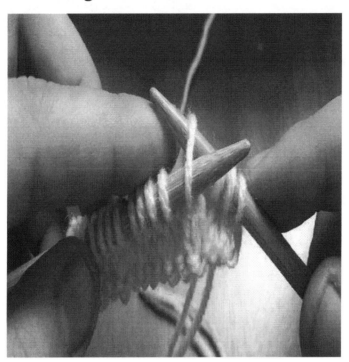

The stitch is then completed as normal, with the yarn being wrapped around the needle counterclockwise. Here the knitter is also holding the working yarn in the left hand, as some knitters prefer:

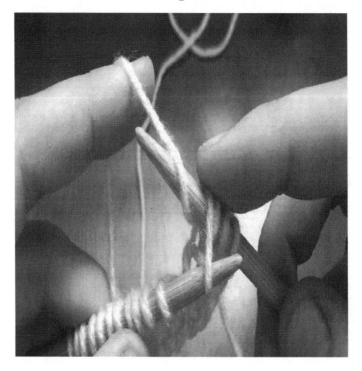

On the next row, the stitch can be worked normally or through the back loop as the pattern directs.

Decreasing: Knit 2 Together and Slip, Slip, Knit

Decreases are useful not only because they shape knitted items but also because they create interesting fabrics. Lace, for example, is made by pairing decreases with increases, which creates a series of holes – lace. The two basic decreases used are the knit 2 together (abbreviated k2tog) and the slip, slip, knit (abbreviated ssk). The difference in the decreases goes farther than simply how they're worked; the k2tog slants to the right, while the ssk slants to the left. This slant is important in shaping items, since a decrease whose slant matches the slant of the fabric gives a more pleasing look in a finished item.

To work the k2tog, the knitter prepares to knit a stitch, but instead of inserting the right needle through the first stitch on the left needle, he or she inserts the right needle through the first two stitches:

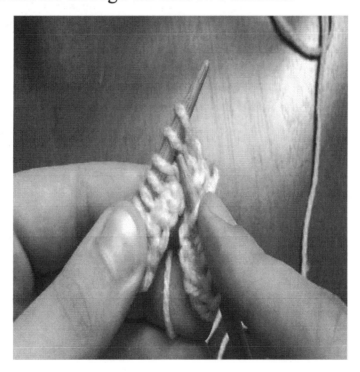

Next, the yarn is wrapped around the right needle counterclockwise as usual. The new stitch is pulled through both of the old stitches, and these are dropped from the left needle:

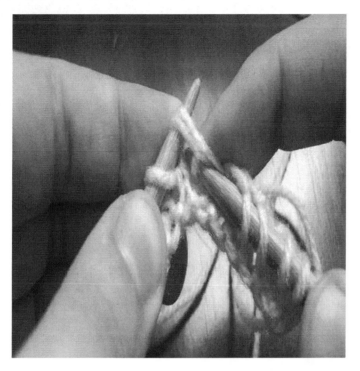

By working this decrease, the knitter has made a single stitch from two stitches.

To work the ssk, the knitter slips the first stitch on the left needle to the right needle as if to knit. Note that the stitch isn't worked, merely slipped. Then, the knitter slips the next stitch on the left needle to the right needle in the same manner:

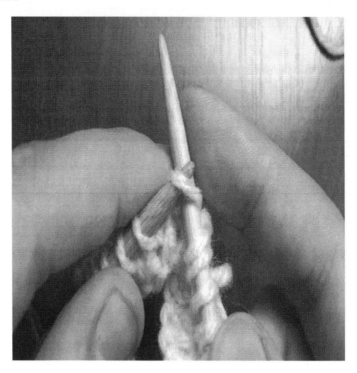

Next, the knitter inserts the left needle into the front loops of the two stitches that are now on the right needle:

Finally, the knitter loops the yarn around the back needle, draws the new stitch through, and drops the two old stitches from the right needle:

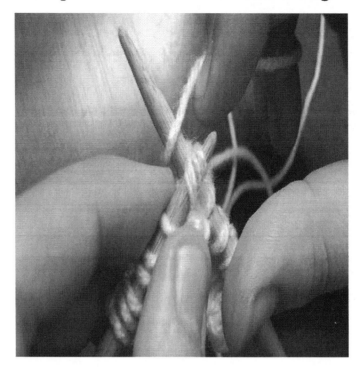

As with the k2tog, two stitches have been decreased down to one stitch.

Increasing: Yarn Over

Increases make knitted fabric wider; as with decreases, there are decorative or 'invisible' increases available, depending on the needs of the project. The yarn over (abbreviated yo) is an open, highly visible increase, and it's the one most often used in lace knitting. Luckily for beginners, it's probably also the easiest to work; although care should be taken to wrap the yarn the correct way on purl rows. Note that in British patterns, the term 'yarn forward' is generally used in place of the term yarn over for those that occur on knit rows, while the term 'yarn over needle' is used instead of the term yarn over for those that occur on purl rows.

To yarn over between knit stitches, the knitter knits to the place where the yarn over will be placed:

Next, the yarn is brought from the back of the work, through the needles, to the front:

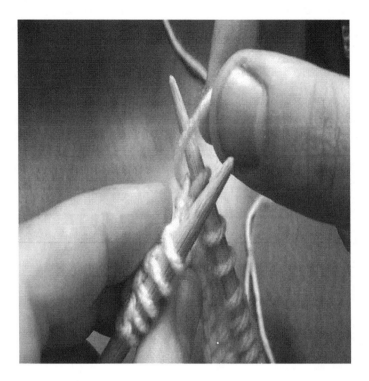

Then, the yarn is wrapped around (over) the right needle:

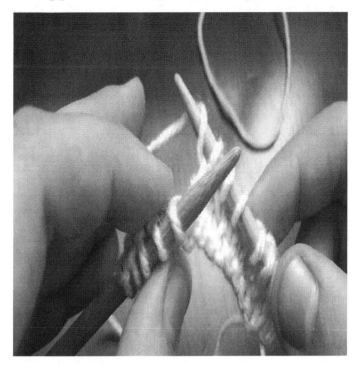

The knitter can now work the next stitch.

To yarn over between purl stitches, the knitter purls to the place where the yarn over will be placed:

The yarn is already at the front of the work, so it doesn't need to be brought forward. Now the knitter brings the yarn over and around the right needle:

The yarn stays in front, and the next stitch is ready to be purled. In this photo, the yarn over from the previous knit row is visible as a small, open hole in the work:

Both methods create one yarn over – the work becomes one stitch wider.

Cables

Cables are created by crossing stitches over other stitches. When the first set of stitches is crossed in front of the second set, the cable will slant to the left; when the first set of stitches is crossed in back of the second set, the cable will slant to the right. In general, the sets of stitches being crossed range in amount from one to five. Any more than five stitches, and the stitches will pull too much, causing the fabric to pucker.

To work a left-leaning cable, in this case a 4-cross, the knitter slips the first two stitches onto a cable needle and holds them to the front of the work:

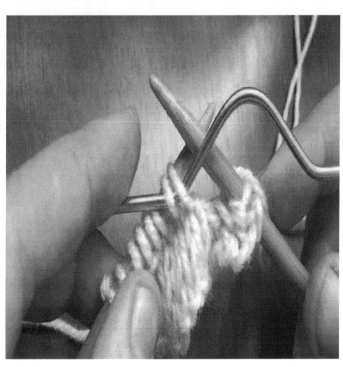

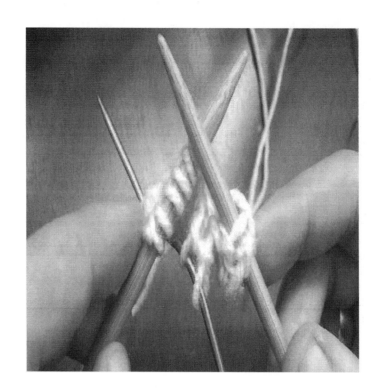

Next, the knitter knits the next two stitches off the left needle, and then knits the two stitches that are on the cable needle. This creates a left-slanting cable in which two stitches have been crossed over two stitches; the term 4-cross indicates that four stitches total are worked.

To work a 4-cross right-leaning cable, the knitter slips the first two stitches onto a cable needle and holds them to the back of the work:

As with the left-cross, the rest of the cable is worked the same: the knitter knits the next two stitches from the left needle, then the two from the cable needle.

Although these examples use knit stitches, it's also possible to cable purl stitches and even to use a combination of knit and purl stitches in one cable. Patterns with cable stitches nearly always include directions for how to work the cables, so it isn't necessary to memorize all types of cables. Knitters who understand the basic principle of how to hold stitches either to the back or front of the work should be able to work most cables, as long as the directions are followed.

Knitting in the Round

Knitting in the round opens up a whole world of possibilities; instead of creating flat fabrics and seaming to create a tube, the knitter simply knits around in a circle to create a tube – no need for seams. Although this may not seem useful for scarf knitting, in actuality, designers are constantly creating new and interesting scarves that are knit in the round. For example, stranded knitting, or knitting with different colors of yarn, can be easier in the round, so multicolored scarves are often knit this way. Round knitting can be done on either circular or double pointed needles; this explanation is for double pointed needles (abbreviated DPNs), the use of which allows knitters to knit small circumferences.

First, the knitter casts onto one needle the number of stitches called for by the pattern:

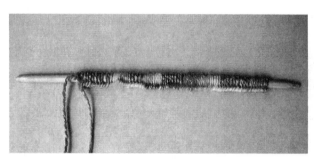

Then, the knitter slips the stitches to the second and third needles, placing an equal amount on each. The stitches should be slipped purlwise:

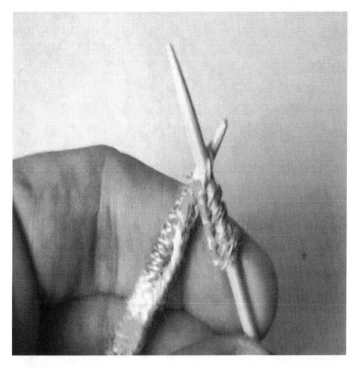

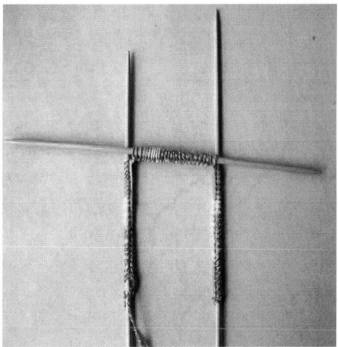

Next, the knitter brings the two 'end' needles together, ensuring that the stitches have not become twisted, and makes the first stitch. The fourth needle is used as the empty needle; the stitch is worked as normal:

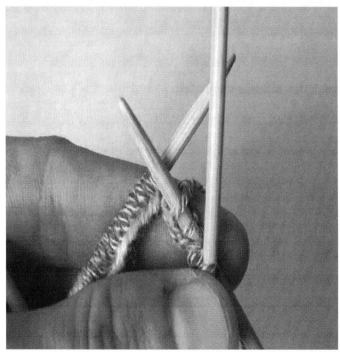

When the knitter comes to the end of the needle, the next needle is worked using the now-empty needle. As the knitter continues to knit the stitches on each needle in turn, a tube emerges:

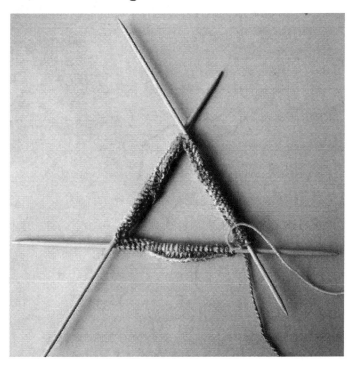

To ensure that the piece isn't knit backwards, the knitter can check that the working yarn is at the beginning of the needle on the right side of the circle before beginning a new round.

Some knitters also find it helpful to knit one row flat (prior to slipping the stitches) before beginning to work in the round. A stitch marker can be placed at the beginning of the first needle to indicate the beginning of the piece.

CHAPTER 3: GAUGE

Gauge refers to the number of stitches and rows over an area of knitted fabric; gauge measurements are generally given in either 1-inch or 4-inch dimensions. A sample gauge measurement, might read '5 stitches and 7 rows to 1-inch in stockinette stitch.' This indicates that if the knitter measures the fabric, each square inch should be made up of five stitches and seven rows, assuming that the fabric is stockinette stitch.

The reason gauge is important has to do with fit; changing the number of stitches or rows per inch changes the size of the finished object. In scarf knitting, this may or may not be of vital importance to the knitter, since scarves are often 'one size fits all.' In other words, if the knitter doesn't work a gauge swatch, and his or her finished scarf is an inch wider than the designer's, this isn't necessarily a crisis. The issue, however, is that gauge is vital with most other projects (sweaters, socks, mittens, etc.), so getting into the habit of getting gauge is ideal. Some scarves, especially lace ones, won't turn out as desired if gauge is off.

Although 'getting gauge' may sound like a waste of time – after all, it's time spent not knitting the actual project – it doesn't have to be. Getting gauge is one way for knitters to learn more about their individual knitting styles as well as to experiment with needle and yarn combinations. Some knitters save their gauge swatches and use them to create patchwork afghans or scarves.

The first step in getting gauge is to take the needles and yarn that will be used for the project and create a square that is at least 4 inches by 4 inches wide. Patterns designate the stitch to be used for getting gauge, which is the stitch the gauge swatch should be worked in. Stockinette stitch is a popular choice.

After the gauge swatch is knit, it should be finished, which means the knitter should bind off. It's often tempting to measure the work while it's still on the needle, but doing so will create a skewed measurement. Once the work has been bound off, it should be washed and blocked. Knitted fabric has a tendency to change size once it has been wet and dried, so this step shouldn't be skipped. To block the piece, the knitter should find a flat, padded surface (such as a mattress or towels laid on a table), then pin the damp swatch into its proper size and allow it to dry completely. The swatch doesn't need to be stretched too tight or bunched up; the fabric should lie flat without being too taut.

Once the swatch is dry, the knitter can unpin it for measuring. Measure how many stitches are in four inches, then divide by four. If there are 30 stitches in four inches, then the stitch-per-inch gauge is 7.5. The row gauge can be found in the same manner. If the gauge is off, which does happen, the knitter should make an adjustment and create a new gauge swatch. A stitch count that is smaller than the one given (for example, 4 stitches-per-inch where 5 are called for) indicates that the knitter should choose a larger needle; a stitch count that is larger than the one given (for example, 6 stitches-per-inch where 5 are called for) indicates that the knitter should choose a smaller needle.

Of course, simply changing the needle size is no guarantee that the proper gauge will be achieved; sometimes it's necessary to change the yarn or even the type of needle (wood versus aluminum, for example). In the case of scarf knitting, a slight deviation from the given gauge could possibly be okay. Therefore, beginners should remain patient in the face of a difficult gauge and view the exercise as practice and a chance to hone skills for future projects.

CHAPTER 4: FINISHING TECHNIQUES

The scarf is knitted. The bind off is complete. The work is done, right? Not necessarily. Before a scarf is ready to be worn, it most likely needs to be blocked. Blocking is the process that settles the finished knitted item into its final shape, sets the stitches into place, and helps give the work a 'hand crafted' rather than 'homemade' look. Some scarves, in fact, absolutely require blocking; lace scarves, for example, generally look like a wad of tangled yarn until blocking 'opens' the holes in the lace and sets the lace pattern. As with creating gauge swatches, the process is relatively easy, although it does add to the amount of time needed to finish a project.

The process for blocking a knit scarf is basically the same process as blocking a gauge swatch. The piece needs to be wet thoroughly, pinned into shape on a flat, padded surface, and allowed to dry. Before pinning the piece, it's helpful to gently wring it in a towel to remove the excess moisture. Be sure to avoid friction and hot water in the case of wool and other animal fibers. When pinning the piece into shape, a tape measure or straight edge can be used to ensure that the edges of the piece are straight.

Another method of blocking that knitters might consider for delicate pieces is the steam method. To perform this method, the first step, wetting the piece, is omitted. Instead, the knitter pins the pieces into the desired shape with the wrong side facing up, then wets a pillowcase or sheet, wrings it thoroughly, and places it on top of the blocked item. Next, the knitter takes an iron and presses the work, ideally using the steam setting and allowing the steam to permeate the piece. When the top layer is dry, the blocking is finished; the piece should be allowed to cool before being unpinned.

For scarves that are far from the desired shape, such as stockinette scarves that are rolling inward, the process can be repeated several times. In these cases, the steam method might be advisable, since the piece can be pinned again and steamed as many times as necessary. It's important to note, that blocking will ease many curling/rolling issues scarves have, generally along the long edges, but adding a border or choosing a different stitch pattern (in the case of knitters who're designing scarves) might be a better option.

Knitted scarves, before being truly finished, may also need some type of embellishment. The ways to embellish scarves are about as varied as knitters themselves; the only thing that can limit embellishments for scarves is the imagination. A few examples of popular finishing embellishments include:

EDGINGS

Edges for scarves can be as simple as a row of single crochet or as complex as a knitted-on row of circles, squares, and more. Designers have created stitch dictionaries dedicated solely to edgings for knit items; well known designer Nicky Epstein, for example, has written not one, but two dictionaries full of edgings, with patterns based on geometric designs, colors, cables, and more.

FRINGE

For a quintessential finishing touch for a scarf, a knitter needs look no further than fringe. Knitters might choose to add fringe to a scarf even when the pattern doesn't call for it; the choice is about personal taste. To create fringe, knitters cut lengths of yarn that are twice as long as the desired fringe length (e.g., for 6-inch fringe, 12-inch lengths). Each is then folded in half so a crochet hook can be used to draw the resulting loop up through the edge of the fabric. The ends of the fringe can then pulled through the loop, creating a knot. For thin fringe, the knitter can place four lengths of fringe to every inch, and for thick fringe, the amount of lengths is only limited by the amount of yarn and space on the edge of the scarf. After all of the lengths are on the scarf, the knitter might trim the ends to ensure they're of uniform length.

TASSELS

Tassels are only marginally more difficult to create than fringe, and they can be joined to the ends of a scarf in the same manner. To create a tassel, the knitter needs a piece of cardboard as tall as the finished tassel will be. Before wrapping the yarn around the cardboard, the knitter cuts a length of yarn and lays it along the top of the cardboard piece. The yarn is then wrapped around the cardboard multiple times; no exact number is right or wrong, knitters can do more wraps for a thick tassel and less wraps for a thin tassel.

Once the yarn is around the cardboard, the knitter can cut the yarn, then remove the cardboard, holding the yarn with the piece that was resting on top. While holding this piece, the knitter wraps another length of yarn (about 6 inches long) around the top of the tassel, about ¼ to ½ of an inch from the top. This length of yarn should be wound around and secured in a knot; the ends can hang down as part of the tassel. The knitter then cuts the strands at the bottom so that they are individual, not loops. The yarn threaded through the top can be tied off and used to join the tassel to the scarf.

EMBROIDERY

Embroidery is a craft in its own right, one with a wide variety of stitches and techniques. Knitters often use embroidery to add pictures or letters to scarves, especially when knitting the colors into the fabric would be cumbersome due to size, shape, etc. One common stitch used for this is the duplicate stitch, which is as simple as adding a layer of stitches (usually in a different color) on top of existing stitches. Stockinette fabric is best for this, as the knitter can mimic the flat Vs of the fabric. Embroidery is also generally added to a knit scarf after the piece has been blocked.

CHAPTER 5: CHOOSING MATERIALS FOR SCARVES

Thanks to the variety of scarf patterns available, virtually all yarn weights and all size needles can be used to make scarves. Thick, chunky yarns and large needles are often used for winter scarves, while delicate, thin yarns and small or medium needles create lacy summer scarves and shawls. The Marylebone Road Scarf pattern by Lion Brand, for example, calls for super bulky yarn and size U.S. 50 (25 mm) needles; at the other end of the spectrum is the Madeira Mantilla by Donna Druchunas, which is made with lace weight yarn and size U.S. 2 (2.75mm) needles. Thin yarn doesn't have to be knit with small needles, nor does thick yarn have to be knit with the biggest needles possible. However, designers and novice knitters alike play and experiment with all weights of yarn on all needle sizes.

Knitters who are new to scarf knitting don't need to feel overwhelmed by variety, because most patterns explicitly outline the type of yarn and size of knitting needles needed. Designers generally call for yarn for their patterns in one of two ways: by brand or by fiber and weight. Needles are given in sizes, British, U.S., or metric, and type (e.g., circular or straight). Knitters often use different materials than required for both aesthetic reasons (to change the look of the scarf) and utilitarian reasons (to get the proper gauge).

Below is an introduction to the main types of yarns and needles used in scarf knitting. Armed with this information, new knitters should be able to not only read the materials requirement section of a pattern, but also to choose, and perhaps substitute materials.

Yarn Brands

Trying to count the number of yarn brands and styles would be akin to trying to count the stars in the sky – the variety is that large. In general, the name of the yarn manufacturer is the same as the brand; most manufacturers produce a range of lines or styles that have their own names. So, for example, Cephalopod Yarns (the brand) produces Bugga (the line). Large manufacturers that produce many types of goods, such as Hobby

Lobby, often have their own brand of yarn. Hobby Lobby's brand of yarn is Yarn Bee, which comes in many styles, including Show Off! Metallic Yarn and Effervesce.

New knitters often wonder whether it's okay to substitute yarn for a pattern using a different brand or line in place of what the designer calls for. As long as the yarn weight and fiber are the same as the yarn called for, there's no reason why a different yarn can't be used. Of course, if the knitter would like to knit a scarf pattern with a yarn that has a vastly different weight or fiber content, he or she should be aware that the gauge and finished product will change. To get the same gauge or finished product in these cases, the needles or pattern itself may need to be changed.

Yarn Weights

Yarn weight can be thought of, most basically, as the thickness of the strand of yarn. The Craft Yarn Council has created a standardized system for yarn weights. The thinnest, finest yarn is designated '0 – Lace' and the bulkiest, fattest yarn is designated '6 –Super Bulky.' Within each weight category there are several types of yarn. The category '4 – Medium' contains worsted, afghan, and aran types of yarn. A pattern might direct the knitter to choose either a Medium yarn or a type of yarn in that category (sometimes both).

To make substitution easier, most yarn manufacturers include the weight and type of the yarn on the ball band. If a scarf pattern calls for a worsted yarn, the knitter can choose any brand or line of yarn that is worsted – as long as the target gauge is hit. Although the Craft Yarn Council (CYC) has created yarn weight categories, discrepancies are still possible between manufacturers, so knitters shouldn't skip gauge swatching.

For a full list of the CYC's yarn weights, their respective types, and average gauges of each, knitters can visit their website at craftyarncouncil.com.

Yarn Fiber Types

As knitting has grown in popularity, the types of materials yarn is made from have grown. While the basic fiber types are still available (acrylic, wool, etc.), manufacturers are now offering yarns made from 'exotic' materials, including banana fibers, qiviut (muskox), and milk protein. Much of choosing a fiber type comes down to personal likes and dislikes as well as budget, although scarf knitters might also consider the drape or wearability of the fiber and how well it responds to blocking. Acrylics tend not to drape or block very well, but are often used because they hold up to multiple washings. For scarves, washing is often not an issue, since scarves aren't subjected to the washing machine with regularity. Wools, wool blends, other animal fibers, and cotton are all popular choices for scarves. They all tend to drape well and respond successfully to blocking.

Needle Materials and Types

Needles can be divided into two categories: materials and sizes or types. Choosing needle materials, much like fiber choice, is mainly about personal preference. Some knitters prefer the warmth of wood or bamboo, while others enjoy the slickness of aluminum or other metals. Knitters who are knitting scarves for the first time might consider choosing needles that aren't too slick, avoiding aluminum, nickel, and some plastics. These often allow the work to move faster, but there's a greater chance of stitches slipping off the tip accidently. Manufacturers make needles from all types of wood, from rosewood to birch; these needles usually create drag on the yarn, making it more difficult for the stitches to slip.

Needle sizes, as with yarn weights, have been standardized by the CYC. In the U.S., most needles are labeled with both a U.S. size and a size in millimeters. A U.S. 8, for example, is 5 millimeters thick. Although most needles are marked in this fashion, it's a good idea to use a needle sizer to check the exact measurement of the needles before starting a project, because discrepancies do happen. A needle sizer is also useful for determining the size of old or unmarked needles.

Related to the size of the needle is the needle type, either straight, double pointed, or circular. Straight needles are used for knitting flat pieces, and manufacturers make them in a range of lengths. For scarf knitting, short lengths (around 6 inches) work well because most scarves are narrow. Scarves that are created by casting on enough stitches for the length of the scarf, on the other hand, require long needles. Circular needles are also used for these types of scarves – knitters can knit on them back and forth without joining the stitches.

Double pointed and circular needles are used for knitting in the round. Tubular scarves that have a small circumference are often knit on double pointed needles simply because most circular needles are too long. Manufacturers do make short circular needles (8 inches or 16 inches in length), but some knitters find these uncomfortable to knit with. Patterns that require the scarf to be knit in the round usually specify double pointed or circular needles as well as the length needed.

CHAPTER 6: TYPES OF SCARVES

Ask someone to describe a knitted scarf, and they'll most likely paint an image of a long, rectangular piece of fabric, perhaps with a design, perhaps knitted in rib. Knitted scarves can be so much more. Below is a listing of the most common types of scarves knitters can find patterns for.

-Rectangular scarf. This is a long, flat rectangle, often with fringe at the ends. While many of these scarves are knit from top to bottom, some are knit side to side. Design elements might include lace, cables, knit and purl patterns, slipped stitches, and more. A general rule for the length of these types of scarves is that they should be as long as the wearer is tall.

-Square scarf. Square scarves are exactly as they sound – a scarf in the shape of a square. Some are knit from side to side, but they can also be knit from corner to corner, using increases and decreases to create the shape. These scarves incorporate the same design elements as rectangular scarves.

-Mobius scarf. A Mobius scarf, sometimes called an infinity scarf, is a scarf in which a twist has been introduced in such a way that the fabric only has one side (although it appears to have two). These scarves are often wide with a small circumference, more like a cowl than a traditional scarf.

-Beaded scarf. Knitters create beaded scarves by knitting beads into the work as they go. The beads can be placed on either side of the work and may be placed randomly or to create a design. Beaded scarves can be any shape.

-Novelty yarn scarf. Perhaps not as popular as they were in the early 2000s, novelty scarves are those made from so-called novelty yarn. This type of yarn usually has nubs or long strands of fiber; common examples include ribbon, eyelash, and boucle. Although many novelty scarves are simple rectangles of garter stitch (since a novelty yarn obscures patterns), they aren't a fantastic choice for absolute beginners since the yarn can be difficult to work with.

-Unique design scarf. The only limit to how a scarf is constructed is imagination. Designers have created scarves of interlocking knit rings, scarves with wavy edges, scarves with purposeful holes in them, and more. Often these are worn for looks rather than warmth.

-Summer scarf. A scarf isn't only for winter. Summer scarves, usually crafted from lightweight yarn in lace patterns, are made to be worn in warm weather as fashion accessories. Many are less wide and long than winter scarves.

-Double knit scarf. Double knitting is a technique that allows the knitter to knit a fabric that is two layers thick. Both sides of this flat fabric are knit at the same time, as opposed to knitting two separate pieces and sewing them together. The technique is often used to create scarves with color designs, since the fabric is reversible. The inside of the scarf hides the messy backsides of the two fabrics, and each side can have a separate design.

CHAPTER 7: TWO TIMES THREE (A RIBBED SCARF PATTERN)

This scarf pattern is broken in to two chapters; the basic pattern and then the detailed pattern instructions.

MATERIALS

-2 skeins King Cole Riot DK (324 yards/294 meters each, 30% wool/70% acrylic) in shade 413

-1 pair size U.S. 8 (5.0 mm) straight knitting needles

-Tape measure

-Large-eyed yarn needle

-Scissors

-Crochet hook

-Stitch marker (optional)

GAUGE

-6 stitches and 7 rows to 1 inch in stockinette stitch

FINISHED MEASUREMENTS

-6 inches wide by 60 inches long. Length can be adjusted for fit.

ABBREVIATIONS

-CO: cast on

-BO: bind off

-k: knit

-p: purl

-k1tbl: knit 1 through the back loop

INSTRUCTIONS

-CO 36 stitches using long-tail cast on. Work 2-row pattern repeat until piece measures 60 inches (or desired length). BO loosely. Weave in yarn ends before adding fringe, if desired.

PATTERN REPEAT

-Row 1: k1tbl, p1, *k1, p1**, repeat from * to ** to last stitch, k1tbl

-Row 2: k1tbl, k2, *p3, k3**, repeat from * to ** to last 3 stitches, p2, k1tbl

FRINGE

-Cut 40 8-inch lengths of yarn (20 for each end). To attach each piece of fringe, fold the length in half and use the crochet hook to draw the folded loop through the bottom edge of the scarf. Gently pull the ends of the folded fringe through the loop and tug to secure. Space the fringe evenly at each end. For thicker fringe, use more lengths; for thinner fringe, use less.

CHAPTER 8: HOW TO WORK THE PATTERN (TWO TIMES THREE)

PREPARATION

Step One: Gather Materials

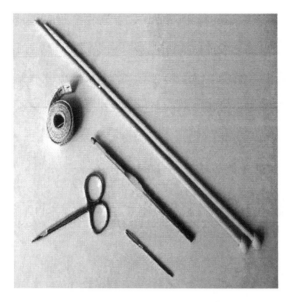

-Needles made from any material are fine for this project. Knitters who don't wish to add fringe will not need a crochet hook.

Step Two: Get Gauge

Casting on 24 stitches should create a 4-inch-wide square for this project; knitters should start with the size 8 needles, but if the gauge is off, refer to the gauge section for help on how to change it. For this project, row gauge isn't as important, since the knitter can knit until the scarf is a suitable length.

KNITTING THE PATTERN

Step One: Cast On

-The long-tail cast on will create one row of garter stitch. Knitters who'd like additional borders at the ends of the scarf might knit three or four rows before beginning the pattern stitch (at the beginning) and binding off (at the end).

Step Two: Work the Pattern Repeats

-This scarf's pattern stitch is relatively straightforward; the stitch at the beginning and end of each row is knit through the back loop, which will create a tighter side edge. The pattern is worked by working the stitches before the asterisks, then repeating the stitches inside the asterisks to the last 1 or 3 stitches in the row. So, for example, the first pattern row would be worked: k1tbl, p1, k1, p1, k1, p1, k1, p1, and so on, until the last stitch, which is a k1tbl.

-Knitters who find it difficult to track whether they're starting row 1 or 2 of the pattern might place a stitch marker on the 'right' side, or the side that is facing the knitter when he or she is about to knit a row 1. When the stitch marker is facing, it's time for the first row of the pattern.

Step Three: Bind Off

This pattern uses the standard bind off; the knitter should bind off in knit, which will match the beginning.

FINISHING AND EXTRAS

Step One: Block

-Blocking will give the stitches extra definition; for help on blocking, see the section on finishing.

Step Two: Add Fringe

-The lengths of fringe can be cut in advance if the knitter is worried about running out of yarn (if he or she desires an extra long scarf). This yarn changes color, so it's possible that the fringe won't match the colors at the end or beginning of the scarf.

CHAPTER 9: ON TO THE NEXT ONE (A STRIPED SCARF PATTERN)

This scarf pattern is broken in to two chapters; the basic pattern and then the detailed pattern instructions.

MATERIALS

-2 skeins Yarn Bee Walk Away sock yarn (231 yards/212 meters each, 40% wool/15% polyamide/45% bamboo from rayon) in Waltz (color one)

-2 skeins Knit Picks Palette (231 yards/211 meters each, 100% wool) in Spearmint (color two)

-1 set size U.S. 2 (2.75 mm) double pointed knitting needles

-Tape measure

-Large-eyed yarn needle

-Scissors

-Crochet hook

-Stitch markers (optional)

GAUGE

-7 stitches and 8 rows to 1 inch in stockinette stitch

FINISHED MEASUREMENTS

-5.5 inches wide by 60 inches long. Length can be adjusted for fit.

ABBREVIATIONS

-CO: cast on

-BO: bind off

-k: knit

-p: purl

INSTRUCTIONS

-Using color one, CO 76 stitches and divide over three double pointed needles for working in the round (25 each on two needles, 26 on one needle). Join for working in the round, being careful not to twist. Place a stitch marker to mark beginning of round if desired.

-Pattern round: k37, p1, k37, p1 (Note: An additional stitch marker can be placed before the first purl stitch if it will aid in remembering to purl.)

-Work pattern round twice with color one. Do not cut yarn. Join color two and work pattern round twice. Do not cut yarn. *Pick up color one and work 2 pattern rounds. Set down color one. Pick up color two and work 2 pattern rounds. Set down color two. ** Repeat from * to ** until work measures 60 inches or desired length, finishing after having worked 2 rounds of color one. Bind of loosely.

FRINGE

-Before adding fringe, the scarf needs to be blocked. Wet the piece thoroughly, then bring to a flat, padded surface to dry. The two purl columns are the sides – the work should be folded at these points. Pin the scarf into shape and allow it to dry completely. Weave in all ends before adding fringe, if desired; don't forget the ends on the inside where the colors were stopped and started.

-Cut 50 8-inch lengths of yarn (25 for each end). For funky fringe, use color one and color two; for plain fringe, choose one color. To attach each piece of fringe, fold the length in half and use the crochet hook to draw the folded loop through both bottom edges of the scarf. Gently pull the ends of the folded fringe through the loop and tug to secure. Space the fringe evenly at each end.

CHAPTER 10: HOW TO WORK THE PATTERN (ON TO THE NEXT ONE)

PREPARATION

Step One: Gather Materials

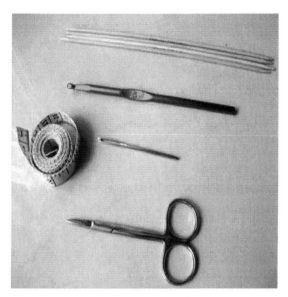

-Knitters who are new to working in the round might choose wood or bamboo needles for this project, as they will grip the yarn and prevent dropped stitches. Because the number of stitches to be cast on isn't too large, either 6-inch or 8-inch long needles will work well. As with the previous pattern, the crochet hook is only needed for adding fringe.

Step Two: Get Gauge

-Twenty-eight stitches should give the knitter a width of 4 inches; as with the previous pattern, row gauge isn't terribly important – the length can be adjusted during knitting.

KNITTING THE PATTERN

Step One: Cast On

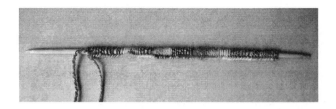

-Cast all of the stitches onto one needle, then slip from the end (the end without the working yarn) until the stitches are divided – 25 on each of two needles, 26 on one needle (since 76 doesn't divide evenly by three).

Step Two: Work the Pattern Repeats

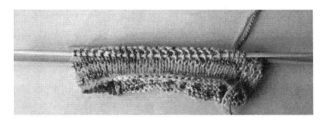

-This scarf is essentially stockinette stitch with two purl stitches as 'seams'; these will make the blocking process easier. Stockinette stitch, when worked in the round, is made by knitting every row. After every two rounds worked in one color, the knitter changes and works two rounds, and so on. Because the number of rows of each color is small, the yarn does not need to be cut and rejoined each time, but care should be taken not to pull the yarn too tight when changing colors.

Step Three: Bind Off

-The standard bind off works fine for this pattern. If the knitter doesn't wish to add fringe, he or she will need to decide whether to sew the ends closed or leave them open.

FINISHING AND EXTRAS

Step One: Block

-Blocking is necessary for finishing this scarf if a flat scarf is desired. It will not only set the stitches, but also flatten the work, setting the purl seams. When blocking, the knitter should take care to 'fold' the scarf at the purl seams. Of course, knitters who like round, tubular scarves might decide not to block the scarf, instead wearing it as is.

Step Two: Add Fringe

-Adding fringe will close the two ends of the scarf and keep them from curling. When bringing the crochet hook through the fabric, the knitter should be sure to catch both sides of the fabric to close the tube. The yarn ends can be incorporated into the fringe or woven in, as desired.

CHAPTER 11: ONE IS THE COZIEST NUMBER (A CABLED SCARF PATTERN)

This scarf pattern is broken in to two chapters; the basic pattern and then the detailed pattern instructions.

MATERIALS

-1 skein Fishermen's Wool by Lion Brand Yarns (465 yards/425 meters, 100% wool) in Natural

-1 pair size U.S. 8 (5.0 mm) straight knitting needles

-Cable needle

-Row counter

-Tape measure

-Large-eyed yarn needle

-Scissors

GAUGE

-5 stitches and 8 rows to 1 inch in seed stitch (Note: To work a gauge swatch in seed stitch, cast on an odd number of stitches, work k1, p1 to last stitch, k1, turn the work, and repeat.)

FINISHED MEASUREMENTS

-6 inches wide by 60 inches long. Length can be adjusted for fit.

ABBREVIATIONS

-CO: cast on

-BO: bind off

-k: knit

-p: purl

-sl: slip

-k1tbl: knit 1 through the back loop

-cl2: cable 2 left (slip 2 stitches to cable needle, hold to front, knit 2, knit 2 from cable needle)

INSTRUCTIONS

-CO 30 stitches using long-tail cast on. Knit 5 rows. Work 6-row pattern repeat until piece measures 59 inches, ending with row 6 of pattern. Knit 5 rows. Bind off loosely, weave in ends, and block.

PATTERN REPEAT

-Row 1: Slip 1, k2, *p1, k1**, repeat from * to ** four times, p2, k4, p2, *k1, p1**, repeat from * to ** 4 times, k2, k1tbl

-Row 2: Slip 1, k2, *p1,k1**, repeat from * to ** four times, p1, k1, p4, k1, *p1, k1**, repeat from * to ** four times, p1, k2, k1tbl

-Row 3: Slip 1, k2, *p1, k1**, repeat from * to ** four times, p2, cl2, p2, *k1, p1**, repeat from * to ** 4 times, k2, k1tbl

-Row 4: As row 2.

-Row 5: As row 1.

-Row 6: As row 2.

CHAPTER 12: HOW TO WORK THE PATTERN (ONE IS THE COZIEST NUMBER)

PREPARATION

Step One: Gather Materials

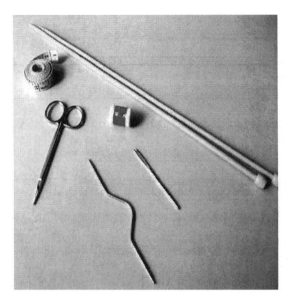

-Knitting needles made from any material are fine for this project. It is advisable to use a row counter to keep track of the row repeats.

Step Two: Get Gauge

-With a stitch-per-inch count of 6, casting on 24 stitches should lead to a 4-inch-wide square. For this project, it's a good idea to achieve stitch gauge; the scarf is designed to look best when the stitches aren't too loose.

KNITTING THE PATTERN

Step One: Cast On

-The long-tail cast on is useful for starting this scarf.

Step Two: Work the Pattern Repeats

-This scarf was created with symmetry in mind. Each edge has 1 stitch for selvedge and 2 stitches in garter, which frames the main pattern. Seed stitch is broken in the middle by a left-slanting cable. Although this may look difficult, it's a simple case of following the stitches one by one in the pattern repeat as with the first pattern in the section. To ensure the cable crosses to the left, the knitter must bring the held stitches to the front of the work:

-Knitters who would prefer a right-slanting cable need only to hold the first 2 stitches to the back instead.

Step Three: Bind Off

-This pattern is bound off in knit.

FINISHING AND EXTRAS

Step One: Weave in Ends

This scarf doesn't require fringe to look 'finished,' although knitters may certainly add some if they desire. Without fringe, however, the yarn ends need to be carefully woven in so that they cannot be seen in the finished project.

Step Two: Block:

The cable in this scarf will 'pop' after blocking, so this step should not be skipped. The knitter should be careful not to stretch the fabric too much during blocking, instead gently pinning the scarf into the shape it naturally would like to hold. As long as the edges are pinned straight, the finished product will look great.

CHAPTER 13: CANDY FANS (A LACE SCARF PATTERN)

This scarf pattern is broken in to two chapters; the basic pattern and then the detailed pattern instructions.

MATERIALS

-4 skeins Knit Picks Palette (231 yards/211 meters, 100% wool) in Orange

-1 pair size U.S. 7 (4.5 mm) straight knitting needles

-Row counter

-Tape measure

-Large-eyed yarn needle

-Scissors

GAUGE

-6 stitches and 8 rows to 1 inch in garter stitch.

FINISHED MEASUREMENTS

-9 inches wide by 60 inches long after blocking. Length can be adjusted for fit.

ABBREVIATIONS

-CO: cast on

-BO: bind off

-k: knit

-p: purl

-sl: slip

-k1tbl: knit 1 through the back loop

-k2tog: knit 2 together

-YO: yarn over

INSTRUCTIONS

-CO 38 stitches using long-tail cast on. Knit 3 rows. Work 4-row pattern repeat until scarf measures 59 inches or desired length. Knit 3 rows, then BO loosely. Weave in ends and block carefully.

PATTERN

-Row 1: Slip 1, k to last stitch, k1tbl.

-Row 2: Slip 1, p to last stitch, k1tbl.

-Row 3: Slip 1, *(K2tog) 3 times, (yo, k1) 6 times, (k2tog) 3 times**, repeat from * to ** once more, k1tbl.

-Row 4: Slip 1, k to last stitch, k1tbl.

CHAPTER 14: HOW TO WORK THE PATTERN (CANDY FANS)

PREPARATION

Step One: Gather Materials

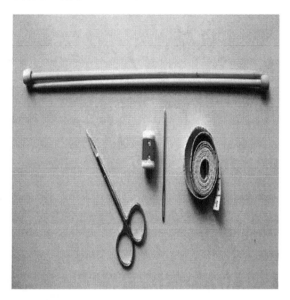

-Although the pattern repeat for this scarf is short, it's advisable to use a row counter, especially for knitters who will be stopping and starting frequently. Knitters who are knitting lace for the first time might choose wood or bamboo needles to prevent the stitches from slipping off.

Step Two: Get Gauge:

-This scarf is designed to 'open' and grow larger after blocking, so obtaining gauge is wise – if the knitter's gauge is significantly larger than what's called for, the finished object may end up resembling a shawl rather than a scarf.

KNITTING THE PATTERN

Step One: Cast On

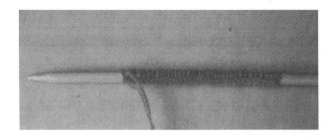

-The long-tail cast on should be used for this scarf; the knit row it produces is incorporated into the design.

Step Two: Work the Pattern Repeats

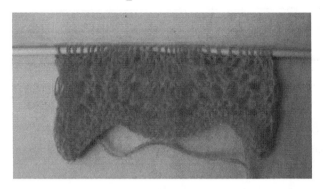

-The pattern repeat for this scarf is fairly simple – mainly knit and purl stitches – but care should be taken when reading the main pattern row, row 3. The parentheses indicate that the stitches inside should be worked the number of times directly after them, while the asterisks indicate the repeat of the pattern across the row. Row 3, then is worked:

-Slip 1, k2tog, k2tog, k2tog, yo, k1, yo, k1, yo, k1, yo, k1, yo, k1, yo, k1, k2tog, k2tog, k2tog, k2tog, k2tog, k2tog, yo, k1, yo, k1, yo, k1, yo, k1, yo, k1, yo, k1, k2tog, k2tog, k2tog, k1tbl.

Step Three: Bind Off

-Here, the standard bind off works fine; the knitter should be sure not to bind off too tightly.

FINISHING AND EXTRAS

Step One: Weave in Ends

-The garter rows at the top and bottom will make it easier to weave in the ends. The knitter can simply match the garter bumps.

Step Two: Block

-This scarf requires careful blocking, so knitters shouldn't worry that it looks limp and messy beforehand. After wetting the scarf, the knitter should gently lay the piece out without stretching it too much – it needs just enough stretch to open the yarn overs. Pin carefully along all four sides or use blocking wires to ensure that the sides are perfectly straight. Let the piece dry thoroughly before unpinning.

Made in the USA
Las Vegas, NV
28 December 2023

83642055R00059